DRINKING·IN·MAINE

DRINKING IN MAINE

50 Cocktails, Concoctions, and Drinks From Our Best Artisanal Producers and Restaurants

MICHAEL SANDERS

PHOTOGRAPHY BY RUSSELL FRENCH

DESIGN BY TOM MORGAN

table
arts
media

Published by Table Arts Media
ISBN-13: 978-0-9844775-1-7
Text Copyright © 2012 by Michael S. Sanders
Photographs © 2012 by Russell French
Cover and interior design by Tom Morgan, Blue Design (www.bluedes.com)
Distributed to the trade by Chelsea Green Publishing
Printed in Lewiston, Maine, USA by Penmor Lithographers

ALSO BY MICHAEL SANDERS

THE YARD: BUILDING A DESTROYER AT THE BATH IRON WORKS

FROM HERE, YOU CAN'T SEE PARIS: SEASONS OF A FRENCH VILLAGE AND ITS RESTAURANT

FAMILIES OF THE VINE: SEASONS AMONG THE WINEMAKERS OF SOUTHWEST FRANCE

ALSO BY MSS AND RF

FRESH FROM MAINE, 2ND EDITION

ACKNOWLEDGEMENTS

We raise a glass to all of the bartenders, restaurateurs, and artisanal producers who helped us make this book possible. Very special thanks go out to our two, in-studio, bartender/cocktail stylists, Roxanne Dragon of Hugo's and Eventide Oyster Company, and Josh Caron, of 555 Restaurant. If you want to understand how and why the art of the local cocktail has had such a meteoric rise, you don't have to look beyond these two thoughtful, knowledgeable, and creative souls. Tom Morgan of Blue Design designed the book cover to cover. Impressive and professional, he's welcome at our table anytime.

NOTES TO THE READER

Turn these pages and you will find cocktails from Maine, yes, but also portraits of **FEATURED ARTISAN PRODUCERS** like Allagash Brewing, Bartlett Spirits of Maine Distillery, and Wyman's of Maine, among others. They are listed in the Index of Featured Artisan Producers at the back of the book, where you will also find an Index of Cocktails by Restaurant to help you find your favorite restaurant's contributions.

ASTERISKED COCKTAIL INGREDIENTS

Immediately following the drinks section, you will find a Glossary of Bar Preps, Simple Syrups, and Infused Alcohols. Whenever you see a special cocktail ingredient marked with an asterisk, the recipe will be found here, in this section.

In loving memory of my father-in-law,
George Albert Russell, a man who knew his way
around an Old Fashioned —Michael Sanders

To the village - may the circle grow ever wider.
—Russell French

CONTENTS

INTRODUCTION

While Maine has been undergoing a culinary revolution with a bright burst of new chefs and restaurants coming onto the national scene and engaging us with incredible dishes drawn from the produce of our farms, forests, and waters, there has been a parallel avant-garde working in the background from another palette altogether.

Those same restaurants and chefs have spawned a bevy of liquid alchemists who have dared to help themselves to the chefs' larder. And just as producers and raisers and fisherfolk and foragers have brought to the table true, authentic, and traditional Maine flavors, so has this small state seen a flowering of distillers, winemakers, cider punks, meaderies, and other daring souls experimenting with everything from potato vodkas to hard ciders, applejack, and pear eau de vies from farmhouse varieties to Kombucha elixir to a New England rum harkening back to the days of sail and the schooner trade.

Maine vodkas, gins, hard ciders, wines, brandies, and meads, these are just the start of a panoply of northern New England ingredients that embraces everything from maple syrup, local sodas, sea salt, and blueberries to rhubarb essence, elderflower syrup, salt-bog cranberries, and goldenrod honey.

And the cocktails? Yes, there's a classic Blueberry Martini and a Hot Buttered Apple Cider. There's a seemingly simple but oh-so-satisfying Back Porch Lemonade, a Cilantro Stinger, a mead and elderflower Summer Sunset, a Gin Pepino. Steaming winter toddies with maple sugar, summer sparklers, new takes on old standards, and old standards made with a local twist—these are just a few of the marvels Maine's barkeeps have created to keep you Drinking In Maine.

—Michael S. Sanders, February, 2012, Brunswick

SPRING

SOMETHING SEXY

- 2-3 OUNCES RASPBERRY SIMPLE SYRUP*
- 1½ OUNCE SWEETGRASS FARM CRANBERRY GIN
- ½ OUNCE DOMAINE DE CANTON LIQUEUR
- DASH OF FRESH SQUEEZED LEMON JUICE
- CRYSTALLIZED GINGER
- LIME PEEL

Chill a martini glass. In a cocktail shaker, put the raspberry simple syrup, gin, Domaine de Canton, and lemon juice. Fill with ice. Shake vigorously, then taste for sweetness, adding more lemon juice if desired. Strain into martini glass. Garnish: take a strip of lime zest, wrap it around a piece of crystallized ginger, and skewer on a thin, bamboo bar skewer.

*   *   *

With its gorgeous hue and wicked aromatic combo of ginger and raspberry against the sere Sweetgrass Farm Cranberry Gin, a Something Sexy will put you right in the mood for one of Chef Henry Ares' accomplished plates. Between the bar, the chef, and the ambiance, **ANNEKE JANS** *quite simply has no competition in Kittery.*

MAPLE TUMNUS

- 2 OUNCES RON MATUSALEM GRAN RESERVA RUM
- 1 OUNCE MAINE MAPLE CLOVE SYRUP*
- ¾ OUNCE FRESHLY SQUEEZED LIME JUICE

Chill a cocktail glass. Put all ingredients in a mixing glass. Fill it with ice. Shake and double strain into the chilled glass. To double strain, use a standard Hawthorne strainer on the mixing glass and pour from that through a tea strainer into the cocktail glass. This beauty needs no garnish.

* * *

As surely as the maple sap begins to run with the first thaw, you'll have a very good chance of finding this on the menu at the BLUE SPOON in the spring. And don't let the brevity of their food and drink list fool you, either. What goes into the glass or onto the plate here can appear deceptively simple—until it hits your mouth and explodes in deliciousness.

FIDDLEHEAD BLOODY

- 4 OUNCES V8 JUICE
- 2 OUNCES TWENTY-2 VODKA OR BEEFEATER GIN
- 1 TEASPOON PREPARED WHITE HORSERADISH
- 2 HEARTY SHAKES CELERY SALT
- 1½ TEASPOONS WORCESTERSHIRE SAUCE
- 4 DASHES ANGOSTURA BITTERS
- GREEN TABASCO AND FRESH GROUND BLACK PEPPER TO TASTE
- ½ TEASPOON: GROUND MUSTARD SEED, GROUND RED AND BLACK PEPPER, COARSE SEA SALT FOR RIM
- WEDGE LIME OR LEMON
- FIDDLEHEAD HOUSE PICKLE* GARNISH (1 CORNICHON AND 1 FIDDLEHEAD FERN, MORE TO TASTE)

Put first 7 ingredients in a cocktail shaker. Shake vigorously. Wet the rim of a pint glass with the citrus wedge, and upend it into a saucer into which you've put the combined mustard, pepper, sea salt, and pepper flakes. Half fill the glass with ice, being careful of rim, and strain contents of shaker over it. Garnish with house pickle of choice, skewered or not.

*   *   *

Laura Albin, GM and co-owner of **FIDDLEHEAD**, *used a family recipe Bloody Mary married with chef and biz partner, Mel Chaiken's, fabulous house pickle featuring the fiddlehead to (re)create a classic that only a Mainer could imagine. Try it and you'll understand why once is not enough.*

[17]

THE REMEDY

- 2½ OUNCES BOOKERS BOURBON
- 1 OUNCE URBAN FARM FERMENTORY GINGER KOMBUCHA
- 1 OUNCE FRESH LEMON JUICE
- 1 OUNCE RHUBARB SIMPLE SYRUP*
- POWDERED GINGER FOR RIM

Chill a cocktail glass. Pour all the ingredients except the powdered ginger into a cocktail shaker and fill with ice. Shake well. Spread the powdered ginger around the edge of a small saucer. Wet the rim of the chilled glass and upend it into the powdered ginger. Fill the chilled glass partway with ice, then strain contents of cocktail shaker into it, being careful not to disturb rim.

*   *   *

50 LOCAL *is as much a popular local watering hole as bistro, though as many come for the full menu of farm-driven favorites as for a small plate or two along with their cocktail. Just like the Remedy, the place is good for what ails you, especially after a long Maine winter.*

GRAPEFRUIT & GINGER

- 2 OUNCES TWENTY-2 VODKA
- ½ OUNCE DOMAINE DE CANTON GINGER LIQUEUR
- 2 OUNCES FRESH-SQUEEZED GRAPEFRUIT JUICE
- CANDIED GINGER

Fill a cocktail shaker with ice. Add the vodka, Domaine de Canton, and grapefruit juice. Combine ingredients until icy cold by moving a mixing spoon rapidly up and down in a chopping motion. Strain into a chilled martini glass, garnishing with a piece of candied ginger.

*   *   *

*Bartender Greg has been coming up with inspired creations to complement Sam Hayward's innovative and award-winning cuisine for almost as long as **FORE STREET** has been around. Stop by on a cool spring night and say hello to a Grapefruit & Ginger to rouse you out of your winter torpor and get the blood flowing.*

BARTLETT MAINE ESTATE WINERY AND SPIRITS OF MAINE DISTILLERY

GOULDSBORO

Nothing exemplifies the Maine artisanal wine and spirit experience more than the Bartlett Maine Estate Winery forty minutes from Bar Harbor. Set on twenty acres of pine and fir on the Schoodic Peninsula, the winery is worthy of every superlative it has accumulated—oldest, largest, most innovative, and, above all, best.

Bob and Kathe Bartlett, two accomplished artists originally from the Midwest, opened their winery in 1983. "A lot of people thought we were nuts when we told them what we were doing," Bob said in his soft drawl. "But then when we opened, we had line of people here out the door and sold out our first wine—3000 bottles of blueberry—in a week and a half."

From there, he never looked back. Today, they make more than a dozen kinds of wine, upwards of 70 thousand bottles, in a pleasingly contemporary facility complete with an airy tasting room of wood and stone. "We're no different than a small California boutique winery," Bob told me, "with stainless steel tanks and barrels of French and American oak—and a lot of passion." They express their passion for this unique landscape not only in their wines, but in their support of the region's blueberry growers and orchardists, with three-quarters of their fruit, and all of the honey used in their mead wines, coming from Maine.

Because Bob is a restless innovator, Bartlett's latest offerings now include two distilled spirits, a Pear Eau de Vie and a Fine Apple Brandy. How good are they? Using a handmade German copper still and French oak barrels for aging, he leaves nothing to chance. The resulting liquid

gold has impressed more than the locals. The Pear Eau de Vie took a Double Gold Medal at the 2011 San Francisco World Spirits Competition while the Apple Brandy brought home a silver—these in competition with more than 1000 offerings from established makers from around the world.

In the tasting room, Kathe offers a wide-ranging and always surprising experience to visitors and small groups. She brings her long experience in tasting along with a low-key, let's-have-some-fun approach that sets the tone for one of the most pleasant hours you can have in the Bar Harbor region. Stop by and maybe you'll be there for the release of Bob's latest experiment: oak-aged rum!

Throughout these pages, you'll find cocktails with Bartlett's spirits, many featuring the Fine Apple Brandy. Kathe can't bear to tamper with the purity of the Pear Eau de Vie.

"It is at its best," she believes, "served from the freezer in a beautiful martini glass simply garnished with a slice of fresh pear and perhaps a mint leaf...."

Bob, on the other hand, prefers a Spirit of Maine Old Fashioned, a streamlined cocktail that allows the essence of the pear to shine through.

BARTLETT MAINE ESTATE WINERY AND
SPIRITS OF MAINE DISTILLERY, GOULDSBORO

SPIRIT OF MAINE OLD FASHIONED

- 1½ OUNCES SPIRITS OF MAINE PEAR EAU DE VIE
- 2 OUNCES BOURBON
- ½ OUNCE SIMPLE SYRUP*
- SPLASH OF FRESH LEMON JUICE
- DASH OF BITTERS
- PEAR SLICE GARNISH

Put the eau de vie, bourbon, simple syrup, lemon juice and a dash of your favorite bitters into a cocktail shaker. Fill with cracked ice. Shake vigorously for 10 seconds. Strain into a cocktail glass. Garnish with a slice of fresh pear.

SWAMP

- 2 OUNCES TWENTY 2 VODKA
- ½ OUNCE MIDORI
- BIG SPLASH PINEAPPLE JUICE
- SPLASH ORANGE JUICE
- 1/3 CHUNK DRY ICE PELLET
- MARASCHINO CHERRY

Chill a martini glass. Fill a cocktail shaker with ice, and add the vodka, midori, and juices. Shake and strain into the chilled glass. Add 1/3 of a chunk of a dry ice pellet. Garnish with a cherry on the rim. Some like to double the vodka content.

*   *   *

Though this drink is named for the primordial vapors that rise off it like a swamp mist in spring, there is nothing rotten in the state of **FROG AND TURTLE** *land. James Tranchemontagne's homey gastropub is a place where the quality of the food and drink is inversely proportional to the pretention—especially after everyone's downed a Swamp or two.*

BASIL GIMLET

- 3 OUNCES COLD RIVER GIN
- ¾ OUNCE CHARTREUSE
- ½ OUNCE ST. GERMAIN
- 1 OUNCE LIME JUICE
- 4–5 LEAVES OLIVIA'S GARDEN BASIL

In a dry mixing glass, muddle basil gently. Add liquors and lime juice. Add ice and shake vigorously. Double-strain through fine sieve into chilled coupe glass.

*   *   *

"The color of this is a fantastic, glowing green," says Roxanne Dragon, *barkeep at* **HUGO'S**. *If you know spring in Maine, we need all the green we can get! The bar, with its own menu and exquisite seasonal cocktails like this one, is a great place to chase away cabin fever with your friends.*

CRANBERRY COSMOPOLITAN

- 1½ OUNCES. STOLI CRANBERRI VODKA
- ½ OUNCE STOLI PERSIK
- ½ OUNCE COINTREAU
- 4 SQUIRTS HOUSE-MADE CRANBERRY SIMPLE SYRUP*
- SPLASH OF FRESH-SQUEEZED ORANGE JUICE
- SPLASH OF FRESH-SQUEEZED LIME JUICE
- SPLASH OF REAL CRANBERRY JUICE
- SPLASH CLUB SODA
- 2-3 FRESH CRANBERRIES
- 1-2 SMALL LIME WEDGES

Put first 7 ingredients into a cocktail shaker. Fill with ice. Shake vigorously. Strain into a chilled martini glass and top with the club soda. Garnish with cranberries and lime wedges.

*   *   *

This gloriously-hued drink, with its tart cranberry and hint of peach, is a happy reminder that warm weather is just around the corner. Bartender Christina Holbrook's creations are just the first step of the warm welcome at **JOSHUA'S,** *carrying over to thoughtful food from the family farm, just as creatively prepared and impeccably served.*

HONEYMAKER MEAD APERITIF

- ½ ounce St. Germain
- 2½ ounces Maine Mead Works Dry-Hopped Mead
- 2½ ounces dry sparkler like cava
- Twist of orange peel as garnish

Chill mead and wine. Pour the St. Germain into a fluted glass, add the sparkling wine and the mead. Twist the orange peel over the glass. Sip.

*   *   *

Elderflower infusions and mead are both ancient preparations newly-discovered and back on our tables. "The floral quality of the mead along with the hops really lends itself to a light, refreshing apéritif," says Elizabeth Lindquist, co-owner of **RED SKY** *with her husband, James. They bring that same thoughtfulness to every aspect of the diner's experience at their restaurant, from a comfortable, relaxed décor to an accomplished, ever-changing menu that will keep you coming back.*

THE BACK RIVER DIRTY MARTINI

- 3 OUNCES SWEETGRASS FARM BACK RIVER GIN
- PINCH OF MAINE SEA SALT
- 4 MARINATED MIXED OLIVES, LIKE ALFONSO AND KALAMATA*

Chill a martini glass by filling it with ice and water. Muddle one each of Alfonso and Kalamata olives and a pinch Maine sea salt in the bottom of a cocktail shaker. Fill glass with ice. Add gin, stir gently, and strain into the chilled martini glass. Garnish with one each Alfonso and Kalamata olives.

*   *   *

Want to soothe your soul? Settle into a window seat at **SHEPHERD'S PIE** *overlooking Rockport harbor at sunset with a Dirty Back River Martini and a sizzling skillet of Chef Brian Hill's Pine Needle Mussels. Sip, have a mussel, repeat.*

BLUEZO

MAKES 2 DRINKS:

- 3 OUNCES WINTERPORT WINERY BLUEBERRY WINE
- 3 OUNCES OUZO SODA FROM LAKONIA, OR OTHER LICORICE SODA
- 1 OUNCE WYMAN'S WILD BLUEBERRY JUICE
- 1 TEASPOON FRESH LEMON JUICE
- 1 TEASPOON FRESH ORANGE JUICE
- 2 ORANGE SLICES FOR GARNISH

Chill two martini glasses by filling them with water and ice. Put all the ingredients except the soda and orange slice in to a cocktail shaker. Add ice and shake 15 seconds. Add soda and stir. Empty martini glasses and strain contents of shaker into the two glasses. Garnish with the orange slices. Variation: put everything but the garnish in a blender, substituting Greek yogurt for the ouzo soda for an other-worldly smoothie!

*   *   *

One of midcoast Maine's best kept secrets, **TRATTORIA ATHENA** *captivates us with an ever-changing blackboard of tantalizing menu choices uniquely inspired by the land and seascapes around it and powered by the two chefs' Greek and Italian origins. They bring each culture's cuisines to life every night, infusing your meal with seasonal and regional delights they've unearthed from select providers.*

ALLAGASH BREWERY

PORTLAND

When you're a Maine craft brewery with a hit product, the pressure to ramp up and crank out the same old brew is intense. Rob Tod, founder of Allagash Brewing in Portland, laughs out loud when he explains the situation.

"Seven years ago, we couldn't *give* our beer away," he says of the now uber-popular Allagash Belgian-style White Ale. "Which is why," he explains, "we'll always have a barrel room where we age our other select brews like Curieux, even though they only represent a tiny part of what we produce."

The barrel room is actually two vaulted spaces packed with over 300 oak barrels, many previously used to age Kentucky bourbon. Take three steps in and inhale, and there's no question—you can almost drink the air itself. You can only imagine what's happening to those very special brews sleeping and steeping in those racks all around you until the day when Rob judges they've matured enough for bottling. Sometimes after 3 *years* in the cask, he puts them back to bed. And all for less than 2% of Allagash's production.

"Yeah," Rob continues, "it may be 1% of our volume, but it's 80% of our culture, what we're about and have always been about, looking for that uniqueness, that innovation, always trying to learn."

What is accepted today, he says, that crisp, dry, super-clean Allagash white, was, way back when, "a total innovation, unfiltered, using Belgian yeast strains and those classic ingredients."

So why mess with a great model? This is why, he continues, "we'll always have a barrel room." And not just a barrel room, but also the 10-gallon pilot batch brew system where any employee—from truck driver to salesperson to marketing manager—can put their hat in the ring, suggesting a recipe that, as

long as it is feasible, the team will execute.

"That's the craft brew tradition!" Tod says. "That's where our Fluxus has come from the last 3 years, and our Black Beer. We have 40 plus totally engaged, passionate people working here, and why not take advantage of all that potential and creativity?"

HABANERO WATERMELON MARGARITA

- 2 OUNCES SILVER TEQUILA
- 1 OUNCE PATRON CITRONAGE
- 1½ OUNCES LIME JUICE
- 1½ OUNCES AGAVE NECTAR
- 1 OUNCE WATERMELON PURÉE
- 3 ONE-INCH CUBES WATERMELON
- 1 SLICE HABANERO, SEEDS REMOVED
- MAINE SEA SALT FOR RIM, OPTIONAL

Make 4-5 one-inch square cubes of ripe watermelon. Purée 2 cubes and put this into a cocktail shaker, muddling with one watermelon cube, habanero slice, agave. Add ice, tequila, Citronage, fresh lime juice, and shake. Salt the rim of a margarita glass, garnish with two watermelon cubes.

*   *   *

While watermelon and habanero at a Maine farmers market are rare birds indeed, once **ZAPOTECA** *made us taste this lush seductress of a drink, we were convinced. Perfect alongside any of the restaurant's smoky, intense wood-grill Oaxacan dishes, especially the carnitas.*

SUMMER WIND

- 1½ ounces Sweetgrass Farm Back River Gin
- 1 ounce Maine Mead Works Honeymaker Lavender Mead
- 1 ounce St. Germain liqueur
- Splash of fresh squeezed lemon juice
- Spritz of jasmine-scented water
- 1 candied rosemary sprig*
- Note: Jasmine-scented water is available at Asian groceries.

Chill a martini glass. In a cocktail shaker, combine first four ingredients, add ice, shake vigorously, strain into martini glass. Garnish with the rosemary sprig.

*   *   *

With just a hint of honey and lavender from the mead, this light refresher will wake you right up after a day in the sun. Order **ANNEKE JANS'** *deep-fried olives to go with, and you'll understand why this restaurant is Kittery's destination dinner venue, and not just in summer.*

GINGER DIESEL

- 6 OUNCES MAINE ROOT GINGER BEER
- 6 OUNCES ALLAGASH WHITE
- ½ OUNCE CRÈME DE CASSIS
- LEMON WHEEL

Pour ginger beer into a pint Pils glass. Add the crème de cassis. Slowly add Allagash white beer, preserving the head. Garnish with a lemon wheel. No stirring required!

*　　*　　*

*At **BAR LOLA**, this just-so summer quaffer has a hint of spice from the ginger beer calmed and deepened by the dry but flavorful Allagash. Let bartender Stella suggest which of her husband, Guy's, Philippino, Hispano, or tutto mondo specials might go well with it....*

THE BARTLETT PEAR COLLINS

- 1½ OUNCES BARTLETT PEAR EAU DE VIE
- ¾ OUNCE SIMPLE SYRUP*
- ¾ OUNCE FRESH LEMON JUICE
- 2 OUNCES CLUB SODA
- 1 LUXARDO MARASCHINO CHERRY
- 1 ORANGE SLICE

Chill a cocktail glass. In a cocktail shaker, put the eau de vie, a simple syrup, and lemon juice. Shake vigorously for 5-10 seconds, then strain into the chilled glass. Add club soda and stir gently. Garnish with the Luxardo cherry and orange slice.

*   *   *

More than 25 years ago, Bob and Kathe Bartlett were among the first in Maine to understand the potential of making local fruit into wine and, today at their **SPIRITS OF MAINE DISTILLERY,** *eau de vies and rum. Using a German copper still and traditional distilling methods then aging in French oak barrels where appropriate, they produce some of the finest alcohols not just in Maine, but in all of New England. "The proof is in the tasting," they say. So come taste!*

CACHAÇA GINGER MOJITO

- 20 FRESH NEW MINT LEAVES
- ½ LIME, IN THIN WEDGES
- 4 OUNCES CACHAÇA, PREFERABLY LEBLON
- 3 OUNCES+/- MAINE ROOT GINGER BREW
- SIMPLE SYRUP, OPTIONAL*

Chill a pint glass. Put the mint leaves into a cocktail shaker then squeeze the lime wedges over the mint, throwing in wedges and muddling gently. Add cachaça and ice and shake well. Pour everything into chilled pint glass, topping with Ginger Brew and ice. Add simple syrup if a sweeter drink is what you want.

*   *   *

Just like the inspired Thai street food at **BODA***, the bar has its own surprises drawn from the Asian palate. Here, ginger, lime, and mint, a common trio in Thai dishes find their way into an incredibly refreshing Mojito. Try it with a couple of apps from the yakitori grills up front and discover heaven on Congress Street.*

MAINE MEAD WORKS

PORTLAND

Mead—honey wine—is one of the oldest alcoholic beverages brewed by man, with various traditions and styles developed across the world from Ethiopia to China to Northern Europe to America. Today, in an old bakery building in Portland, Ben Alexander's Maine Mead Works is bringing to life new-style offerings which take their inspiration from locally-sourced wildflower honeys gently infused with the seasonal bounty of our region. This means meads offered each in its season, uniquely and subtly married with local blueberry, lavender, apple, elderberry, strawberry, even maple.

At the meadery, two steps into the fermenting room, and your eye is drawn to four clear glass columns rising 8 feet against one wall and filled with honey-colored liquid. "This is our continuous fermentation line," Alexander explains proudly. "Garth Cambray, a South African scientist who knows more than almost anybody about mead, designed it with us inspired by an African traditional technique. Honey and water go in one end and move slowly through the system, the yeast converts the natural sugars to alcohol." Then it will finish its fermentation in tanks. While some meads mature in two months, others may rest several years in old bourbon barrels, before bottling.

"Our process helps produce a dry, light mead which retains more of the subtle flavors of the Maine wildflower honey we use as a base," Alexander says. "We marry that to local ingredients following the seasons, strawberry mead in July, and apple mead called cyser in September, a cranberry mead in November." And they're always experimenting, like their reserves—Coffee Maple, Spiced Mead.

"We make a mead that appeals to the wine drinker who's looking for something new, but something local, interesting. It has to be light but also complex enough to drink with food." Traditional meads can be sweet, but Alexander's are dry indeed, making the experience in nose and palate remarkably like drinking dry white wine, with a delicate overlay of fruit and floral aromas depending on the mead.

Light and complex just begin to capture Maine Mead Works' offerings, and you're sure to come up with your own words to describe this unexpected taste of Maine in a bottle.

CILANTRO STINGER

- ✦ FRESH SQUEEZED JUICE OF HALF A LIME
- ✦ 1 OUNCE KETEL 1 CITRON VODKA
- ✦ 1 OUNCE COLD RIVER GIN
- ✦ 2 TABLESPOONS FRESH CILANTRO, WHOLE LEAVES AND STEMS
- ✦ DASH OF SIMPLE SYRUP OR TASTE
- ✦ 2 DASHES FLAVORLESS HOT SAUCE LIKE FROSTBITE

Combine ingredients over ice in a cocktail shaker and shake vigorously. Strain into a chilled martini glass and garnish with a sprig of rosemary.

* * *

Zara Edwards, the bar manager at CAIOLA'S *in Portland, loves the way the lime, cilantro, and hint of heat turn this into a real refresher. Try her Cilantro Stinger when the thermometer climbs. At the restaurant, there's absolutely nothing finer than spending a summer evening out on the fabulous patio, sipping a cold Stinger and enjoying some fine, local food with family or friends.*

BASIL RICKEY

- 2 OUNCES RASPBERRY-INFUSED VODKA*
- I TABLESPOON BASIL SIMPLE SYRUP*
- I TABLESPOON FRESH-SQUEEZED LIME JUICE
- POLAND SPRING SELTZER WATER
- LIME WEDGE
- I-2 FRESH RASPBERRIES

In a cocktail shaker, put the vodka, basil simple syrup, and lime juice and shake. Fill a Collins glass half full of ice, pour in contents of shaker, top with seltzer. Garnish with a lime wedge and a raspberry or two.

*   *   *

A person could be very, very happy for a very, very long time at either of the two bars, one downstairs and intimate, the other upstairs and roomier, that make up **EAST ENDER**, *our vision of what the perfect watering hole slash gastropub might look like. Small plates, artful, seasonal cocktails like the one above, genial help—are we missing something?*

GIN PEPINO

- 2 OUNCES SWEETGRASS FARM BACK RIVER GIN
- 2 THIN SLICES CUCUMBER (MAINE GROWN IN THE SUMMER)
- 2 THIN SLICES LEMON
- 6 OUNCES CUCUMBER SODA (AVAILABLE IN SPECIALTY MARKETS)

Fill a cocktail shaker half full with ice, add the gin and stir gently. Put the cucumber and lemon slices in a short glass and strain the gin over them. Fill to top with cucumber soda.

*   *   *

EL CAMINO *always makes everything they do look so easy. Of course, it takes the right gin and a gentle hand and so many other things (usually unseen) to pull off not just this breezy refresher, but everything else they do so well. Stop by and find out for yourself.*

CLAM SHOOTER

- Shooter Party Quantity – 12 Shooters
- 5½ ounces tomato juice (one small can)
- 4 ounces Bar Harbor Clam Juice
- 2 teaspoons prepared horseradish
- 1 tablespoon lemon juice
- 3-4 dashes Worchestershire sauce
- 5-6 dashes hot sauce
- Pinch Maine Sea Salt and pinch black pepper
- 9 ounces tequila or vodka
- 1 dozen Mahogany or Littleneck clams

Combine everything except the vodka or tequila and the clams in a quart container with a cover. Stir. Taste. Adjust seasonings. Add tequila or vodka. Chill, covered, at least 3 hours, preferably overnight. To serve, pour 1½ ounces of mix into each shot glass. Open clams without losing the liquid inside, and serve 1 alongside each shooter to pour into the glass and take down in a gulp.

*   *   *

This Clam Shooter takes its inspiration—and its flavors—straight from the briny deep, just like the **EVENTIDE OYSTER COMPANY.** *Owned and run by the Hugo's team right next door, Eventide takes the raw bar experience up a notch or ten.*

BLUEBERRY THYME LEMONADE

- 1 TABLESPOON WYMAN'S FROZEN BLUEBERRIES, THAWED
- 1 OUNCE THYME SIMPLE SYRUP*
- 2 OUNCES BLUEBERRY VODKA
- JUICE OF 2 LEMONS
- 2 TABLESPOONS WYMAN'S BLUEBERRY JUICE
- LEMON WEDGE FOR GARNISH
- THYME SPRIG FOR GARNISH
- 2 BLUEBERRIES FOR GARNISH

Chill a highball glass. In a cocktail shaker muddle blueberries and thyme simple syrup. Fill a cocktail shaker with ice, add vodka, lemon, and blueberry juice. Shake vigorously and serve in the highball glass. For a garnish, skewer the blueberries on the thyme sprig and use the lemon wedge to hold the skewer to the side of the glass.

*   *   *

This is the drink to enjoy on one of those last days of summer, when the days are warm and the nights have that first hint of chill. As a prelude to one of **FISHBONES AMERICAN GRILL'S** *thoughtful and accomplished meals, there is nothing so perfect as a first course before the first course, so to speak, opening the mind and palate to everything to come.*

STRAWBERRY LAVENDER MARGARITA

- Bar salt
- 1½ ounces strawberry-infused tequila*
- ½ ounce lavender-infused triple sec*
- ½ ounce lemon juice
- ½ ounce lime juice
- ½ ounce simple syrup
- Strawberry

Wet the rim of a martini glass and dip in the bar salt. Put the tequila, triple sec, lemon and lime juice, and simple syrup into a cocktail shaker. Fill with ice. Shake briefly then strain into the martini glass, garnishing with a fresh strawberry.

*   *   *

Come July in Maine, nothing shouts summer like fresh farmers' market strawberries, here at the bar of Portland's **FIVE FIFTY FIVE** *restaurant infused in tequila. This margarita, with an order of Chef Corry's Bang Island Mussels with Roasted Garlic and Pickled Peppers, reminds us why our state's motto is "The way life should be."*

WYMAN'S OF MAINE

MILBRIDGE

In 1874, Jasper Wyman established a cannery in his hometown of Milbridge, Maine producing cans of sardines and clams. By 1900, he was harvesting and canning the local wild blueberries that grow naturally on large swaths of land called barrens—formed by receding glaciers on the Atlantic coast.

The Wyman family understood from day one that they could not "farm" wild blueberries. Instead, the family became wild blueberry caretakers, nurturing the low bushes and protecting the unique, natural environment where the precious berries thrive. Long ago, Wyman's embraced the modern principles of sustainability and environmental stewardship. And today, they are committed to strict water conservation, recycling, composting, and employee and community health programs. They also invest in ongoing pollination research to better

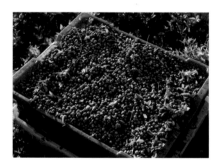

understand the honeybees that are so crucial to the survival of crops around the world.

Though Native Americans had long ago discovered the natural goodness of the wild blueberry, even attributing healing and magical powers to it, it wouldn't be until the 20th century when scientists began to realize that there was a whole world of good in that one little berry.

They are sweet and delicious, yes, but wild blueberries are also packed with powerful antioxidants. In fact, wild blueberries have more antioxidant capacity per serving than many other fruits. And antioxidants may promote health by preventing certain kinds of cell damage associated with aging and progressive diseases.

Individually flash frozen within hours of harvesting, Wyman's wild blueberries

can be stored in your freezer for up to two years. A whole serving of the USDA's 5-A-Day program is just a half cup. You'll love them in smoothies, on cereal, or simply as a snack. Wyman's juices—always 100% juice!—are also an easy and delicious way to get healthy fruit into your family's diet.

Today, Maine harvests 99% of all wild blueberries in the US, with Wyman's taking its place as the #1 harvester, packager, and seller of the crop. While home cooks have long appreciated the wild blueberry, amateur mixologists and professional barkeeps are discovering just how much they can bring to a cocktail. Mix up that summer barbecue by serving Oxford House's Maine Blueberry Martini or a pitcher of Blueberry Thyme Lemonade from Fishbone's American Grill. Cheers!

2 TIMING ROSE

- 1 TABLESPOON BEACH ROSE PETALS
- ROSEMARY-INFUSED HONEY*
- 2¼ OUNCES SWEETGRASS FARM 3 CROWS RUM
- 1 OUNCE FRESH LIME JUICE
- SPLASH ORANGE JUICE
- SPLASH MAINE ROOT GINGER BREW
- SPRIG OF ROSEMARY
- LIME WEDGE
- LEMON TWIST

Muddle beach rose petals and honey in the bottom of a tall high ball glass. Add ice, rum, lime juice, and orange juice and top with a splash of the ginger beer. Garnish with a lime wedge, sprig or rosemary, and lemon twist.

*   *   *

Fragrant pink and white beach roses are a common sight on Maine's rocky coast. Along with all things from the sea on the regular menu, Chef Brian Hill has brought their petals, with a hint of rosemary and lime, into this take on that classic Jamaican ginger beer cocktail. Take a sip, breathe deeply, and contemplate the wonders that await you on **FRANCINE BISTRO'S** *menu.*

BLACK PEPPER PLUM MOJITO

- 1½ OUNCES FRESH RED PLUM, DICED
- 4 BLACK PEPPERCORNS
- 5 MINT LEAVES
- 1 TABLESPOON SUGAR
- 4 OUNCES SWEETGRASS FARM 3 CROWS RUM
- SELTZER
- LIME SLICE GARNISH
- PLUM SLICE GARNISH
- SUGAR FOR RIM OF GLASS

Sugar the rim of a highball glass. In the bottom of the glass, muddle the fresh plums, peppercorns, 4 mint leaves, and sugar until all ingredients are crushed and well mixed. Add the rum, fill with ice, and top with seltzer. Stir. Serve with plum, lime, mint leaf garnish.

*   *   *

Just because **THE FROG AND TURTLE** *is so comfortable and casual, don't think they're not full of suprises, like combining black pepper, mint, plum, and rum to make this knock-your-socks-off mojito. Put one down with a side or two of their abfab gastropub fare, however, and you'll believe these guys are capable of anything, pretty much.*

BEE SHANDY

- 7 OUNCES ALLAGASH WHITE ALE
- 4½ OUNCES GREEN BEE LEMON STING SODA
- 1½ OUNCES LEMON-ROSEMARY VODKA*
- ROSEMARY SPRIG FOR GARNISH

Put a small handful of cracked ice into a pint glass. Add 7 ounces of Allagash White then the soda and float the vodka on top. Do not mix. Garnish with fresh rosemary sprig.

*   *   *

You can have a great, largely local meal at **FRONTIER**. *Ditto drinks. Or see a show, movie, performance, or art opening in the back space. Or just drink in the view of the Androscoggin River crashing over the dam as you eat. It is all part of founder Michael Gilroy's vision of a place where everything is inspired by the world, where you can find a feast for all of the senses, and, very likely, a lot of folks who are also there along for the journey.*

SUMMER SUNSET COCKTAIL

- 2½ ounces Fiddler's Reach Mermaid's Song Mead
- ½ ounce St. Germain elderflower liqueur
- 1 teaspoon fresh squeezed lemon juice
- Generous splash of prosecco
- Orange twist for garnish

Combine first 3 ingredients over ice in a cocktail shaker and shake vigorously. Strain into a chilled martini glass and then add the prosecco. Garnish with an orange twist.

*   *   *

The Summer Sunset cocktail was born at **JOSHUA'S RESTAURANT** *in Wells when bar manager, Kristina Holbrook, was inspired by two warm, sunny, slightly old-fashioned flavors—elderflower and honey. There's nothing old-fashioned about Chef Josh Mather's cooking, however, except the belief that fresh and local is best. Good thing the family farm is just down the road.*

BACK PORCH LEMONADE

- 1½ OUNCES VODKA
- 3 OUNCES LEMON JUICE
- SPLASH OF CRANBERRY JUICE
- SPLASH OF MAINE ROOT GINGER BREW
- 1 OUNCE+ GINGER SYRUP*
- 1 PIECE CANDIED GINGER
- 2-3 BLACK PEPPERCORNS

In a pint glass, combine first 5 ingredients with ice, stir. Adjust sweetness with more ginger syrup. Garnish with the peppercorns and candied ginger.

*　　　*　　　*

A fresh take on summer's all-time favorite drink, lemonade from our friends at **SEAGRASS BISTRO**. *For a non-alcoholic drink, just substitute seltzer for the vodka.*

Check out their new location (and new full bar!) on Route 1 in Yarmouth. Their menu changes every 3 weeks to reflect local seasonal produce with nightly specials and prix fixes as well.

BAR HARBOR FOODS

EAST MACHIAS

When husband and wife team, Mike Cote and Cynthia Fisher, took over Bar Harbor Foods nearly a decade ago, it was with the intention to gently transition this long-time Downeast Maine company from one family's hands to their own. Considering the line of traditional canned fish, chowders, stocks, fancy seafood, and New England traditional preparations that was the Bar Harbor line, they faced a special challenge. "Why," Mike says, "radically remake everything? Better to return the company to its roots, and to celebrate what was so great about those maritime traditions in some new offerings for more contemporary tastes, too."

One of the unique attributes of their products—aside from using the best, truly local ingredients and simplest preparations—is that they require no additives or preservatives. "They taste only of what's on the label," says Cynthia, "of the cold and clean Maine waters they come from. Who can improve that? Who would want to?"

Today, knowing where your food comes from, that it is as sustainably harvested as possible, that the company who makes it is a good environmental steward and community partner—these are all more important than ever.

At Bar Harbor Foods, Mike and Cynthia employ two dozen full time people at their cannery in Whiting. Where the lobstermen used to beach their boats in early winter at season's end, now they're going out for the sweet, winter Jonesport clams that will enrich the company's stocks, sauces, and bottled juice. The lobster Bar Harbor uses is sustainably-trapped, certified Maine lobster and their sardines, mackerel and herring wild-caught. Whenever they can use a Maine product like maple syrup or Raye's mustard, they proudly boast of it.

Think that "traditional" means stodgy or old-fashioned? Sure, Bar Harbor Foods

is proud to offer a varied line of chowders, bisques, and seafood sauces. But they've been hard at work bringing a few, well-chosen, gourmet inspirations to the table, too.

"For a healthy change from bacon on Saturday morning," Cynthia says, "try our smoked sardines with maple glaze along with your eggs for breakfast." Herring in Cabernet Wine Sauce or Tomato Basil Sauce or with Raye's Stoneground Mustard— these can spice up any cocktail party or, with just a garnish or two, become an easy, impressive dinner party first course. To complement, for the cocktail serve the Eventide Oyster Company's Clam Shooter with Bar Harbor clam juice, and taste the ocean in every drop.

FRESH CILANTRO MARTINI

- 5 OUNCES VODKA
- JUICE OF ½ LIME
- ¾ OUNCE CILANTRO SYRUP*
- PINCH OF FRESH CHOPPED FARMERS' MARKET CILANTRO
- BARSPOON FULL OF FINE SLICED FRESNO OR OTHER HOT PEPPER

Chill a martini glass by filling it with ice and water. Put the fresh cilantro, pepper, and cilantro syrup in a cocktail shaker. Fill with ice. Add the lime juice and vodka and shake vigorously. Strain into the chilled martini glass. Garnish with a few slices of the fresh pepper and a cilantro sprig.

*   *   *

This martini is capable of the impossible: cooling you down and heating you up all at once and with an explosion of flavors rarely met in a single drink. It is the perfect preparation for the wonders that will follow during your meal at **SHEPHERD'S PIE**, *where Brian Hill works his magic against one of Maine's most beautiful backdrops.*

COLD RIVER SHIVER

- ½ ounce Cold River Vodka
- ½ ounce Bacardi Rum
- ½ ounce Bombay Sapphire Gin
- ½ ounce Milagro Tequila
- ½ ounce Cointreau
- Cranberry-Lime Seltzer
- Lime wedge garnish

Fill a martini glass with ice and water. In a cocktail shaker, combine all ingredients over ice except the seltzer and lime wedge. Shake vigorously. Dump martini glass contents and fill with contents of strainer, topping off with the seltzer and garnishing with the lime wedge.

*   *   *

You don't have to be a shipwright coming off a long shift at the Bath Iron Works shipyard just down the street from **SOLO BISTRO** *to develop a thirst after a long summer's day outdoors. Come down into Solo's cool bar, pull up a stool, and discover the Shiver.*

BHF CLAM SHACK MARGARITA

- 2 OUNCES BAR HARBOR FOODS CLAM JUICE
- 2 OUNCES TEQUILA
- 2 OUNCES LIME JUICE
- ½ TEASPOON AGAVE NECTAR
- COARSE KOSHER SALT FOR THE RIM, PREFERRED
- 2 LIME WEDGES

Chill a martini glass, stemless or not. In a cocktail shaker, put the clam juice, tequila, lime juice, and agave nectar. Fill the shaker with ice, shake 5 seconds until slightly frothy. Spread the salt around the edge of a small saucer, then wet the rim of the chilled glass with a lime wedge. Upend the glass in the salt to coat rim. Pour contents of shaker carefully into chilled glass. Garnish with lime wedge.

* * *

Leave a food photographer alone in his studio surrounded by cocktail supplies long enough, and something unexpected is sure to happen. Like here. Refreshing - sea foam on top, nice lime flavor with ocean undercurrent and a good helping of iron with your tequila. Like a swim off the Maine coast. Brisk. Refreshing. Reminds you that you're alive.

BLUEBERRY COSMO

- 1½ OUNCES BLUEBERRY VODKA
- ¾ OUNCE ORANGE LIQUEUR
- ½ OUNCE LIME JUICE
- ½ OUNCE BLUEBERRY COULIS*
- SPLASH CRANBERRY JUICE
- LIME WHEEL FOR GARNISH

Chill a cocktail glass. Put vodka, orange liqueur, lime juice, blueberry coulis, and cranberry juice into a shaker. Top with ice and shake vigorously. Strain into the cocktail glass, and garnish with the lime wheel.

*   *   *

The bold, clean flavors of this Maine-tinged Cosmo are typical of Chef Lee Skawinski's approach to making you happy at **VIGNOLA'S**. *Keep it simple. Keep it authentic. Get inspired by what's around you. Follow the seasons. Have fun.*

FALL

CAMPFIRE MARTINI

- 4 SPRIGS APPLE MINT
- 1½ OUNCES SMOKY APPLE-INFUSED TWENTY 2 VODKA*
- 1-2 TEASPOONS SMOKY LEMON SIMPLE SYRUP*
- 2 OUNCES URBAN FARM FERMENTORY BABY JIMMY HARD CIDER
- 1 SLICE GRILLED LIBERTY APPLE

In a pint glass, muddle the sprigs of mint with ice. Pour in the infused Twenty 2 vodka, the hard cider, and last, smoky lemon simple syrup. Shake well and strain into a martini glass. Float a thin slice of grilled apple on top for garnish.

*   *   *

*This architected cocktail, with Urban Farm's unusual hard apple cider echoed in the vodka, sweet smoky syrup, and garnish, captures all you have to know about **EAST ENDER**. Unusual. Original. Satisfying. And we haven't even talked about the food! (Just as good as the drink, equally locally inspired and fueled.)*

HOT BUTTERED APPLE CIDER

- Après Ski Party Quantity: 6-8 drinks
- ½ gallon Maine apple cider
- 2 small oranges, halved and sliced thin
- 4 ounces butter
- ½ cup brown sugar
- 10-12 cinnamon sticks
- 1½-2 cups Bartlett Fine Apple Brandy

Reserve 8 half-slices of orange. In a large saucepan over medium heat, melt the butter and add orange slices and brown sugar, cooking until slices caramelize. Add contents of pan to the apple cider along with the cinnamon sticks and heat gently until steaming. Add the apple brandy. Pour into glass mugs and garnish with an orange slice and a cinnamon stick. Substitute quince slices for a truly unique drink.

*　　*　　*

FIDDLEHEAD *barkeep and co-owner Lisa Albin knows her way around the stove as well as the bar. Here, she shows just how much joy the sacred marriage of Maine apple cider, butter, and oranges with Bartlett's Fine Apple Brandy can bring to the palate.*

SWEETGRASS FARM WINERY AND DISTILLERY

UNION

After a career largely spent making wine for others, in 2005 Keith Bodine settled into Sweetgrass Farm with his wife, Constance, and their three young children. Soon after, they opened the doors of their own winery and distillery, offering fruit wines, a distinctive gin, and a cranberry port. Apple brandy, rum, whiskey, a maple-infused spirit, and two kinds of bitters soon followed. Their products now number 18, with a clientele far beyond those who venture off Route 1 to discover their storybook New England, 70-acre farm spread on the Medomak River.

Just three years later, their Back River Gin would take its place on Wine Enthusiast's Top 50 Spirits of 2008, with the judges being most impressed by its incredible expression of flavors.

To Constance, that's no accident. "Our gin tastes like Maine," she says simply. "You can taste this place in our gin, the ocean and the pine trees and the blueberry barrens, the sea air."

If two keys to capturing such ephemeral essences are Keith's skill as a distiller and his wife's as a taster, one further is certainly the still itself. "We looked at mostly German stills until," says Keith, "we found this one, a basic alembic pot still from Portugal that preserves the flavor of what you're distilling." With local blueberries, cranberries, apples, and other base ingredients, they know they're starting with the best. The rest is up to them.

At their bucolic tasting room built right into the distillery, all of those flavors come alive in your glass, whether it is that award-winning gin or a bracing apple brandy or a smooth-sipping fruit wine. It's no surprise that they see the same faces stopping in, and not just their neighbors.

And now, with wider—justified—acclamation for their labors, they're getting attention from the rest of the country as well. Come by and visit. Taste. Enjoy.

SPICY HERBED TOMATO WATER MARTINI

- 3 Olivia's Garden basil leaves, in chiffonade
- 3 ounces tomato water*
- 2 ounces gin
- Juice of a lemon wedge + 1 lemon wedge
- Maine Sea Salt Company Lemon Sea Salt
- Celery stalk sliver for garnish
- Lemon wheel for garnish

Fill a nonmetallic mixing glass with ice, add tomato water and slivered basil and stir to incorporate. Add gin and lemon juice. Shake vigorously and strain into a chilled martini glass rimmed with lemon sea salt. Garnish with celery sliver and lemon wedge.

*   *   *

Don't let **FISHBONES'** *blue collar location fool you. This is one of the best bars in Maine, with a kitchen to match. The tomato water is simple, elegant, and gives this martini a distinctive punch making the most of those early fall tomatoes.*

GOLDEN DELICIOUS SCOTCH SOUR

- 2 OUNCES FRANCINE BISTRO SOUR MIX*
- 2 OUNCES INFUSED GOLDEN DELICIOUS SCOTCH*
- MINT LEAF
- LEMON WHEEL
- THIN WEDGE OF GOLDEN DELICIOUS OR OTHER APPLE

In a cocktail shaker, put the sour mix and Golden Delicious infused scotch. Fill with ice and shake. Pour this into a cocktail snifter over fresh ice. Garnish with the lemon wheel, laying the mint leaf and apple wedge on top of the ice.

*   *   *

FRANCINE BISTRO *creates seasonal infusions starting in the spring, with dandelion leaves and flowers to liven up their bar offerings. That same care and attention to local flavors goes into everything they do, from first bite and sip to last. They use local Golden Delicious apples here for their distinctive flavor and scent, that hint of almost banana-pineapple that, together with the citrusy sour mix, makes this an otherworldly sipping experience.*

'RITA HAYWORTH

- 2 OUNCES ANCHO PEPPER/HIBISCUS FLOWER INFUSED TEQUILA*
- 1 OUNCE COINTREAU
- 4½ OUNCES HOUSE-MADE SOUR MIX*
- 4 LIME WEDGES
- 1 TEASPOON GRYFON RIDGE SALISH SMOKED SALT FOR RIM
- ¼ TEASPOON COARSE KOSHER SALT FOR RIM

In a small saucer, mix the salts, then spread to the edge where the rim of the glass will touch. Use one of the lime wedges to wet the rim of a stemless or regular martini glass and upend into salt. In a cocktail shaker, put the tequila, Cointreau, sour mix, squeeze 3 lime wedges, add them, add ice, and shake vigorously. Strain into the martini glass. Garnish with lime wedge.

*   *   *

FRONTIER *is a generous, light-filled space built into one corner of an old textile mill overlooking the Androscoggin River,, and also a great place to hang, 'Rita Hayworth in hand, bowl of steaming mussels and local charcuterie plate in front of you. There is a long bar, open seating tables with those dramatic views, and then, tucked away, an art gallery/cinema/ performance space featuring eclectic film, poetry, live music, and other entertainment. Or you could just have another 'Rita and enjoy the view with your dinner.*

COLD RIVER MAINE BLUEBERRY MARTINI

- 2½ OUNCES BLUEBERRY VODKA
- I OUNCE BLUEBERRY-THYME SYRUP*
- 4 WYMAN'S MAINE BLUEBERRIES
- I TEASPOON SUPERFINE SUGAR

First skewer 4 blueberries on a bamboo cocktail pick. Dip the skewer into cold water, shake off excess gently, and roll in the superfine sugar spread shallowly on a saucer. Freeze at least 10 minutes. Fill a cocktail shaker with ice and add the vodka and blueberry-thyme syrup. Shake vigorously for 10 seconds. Strain into a chilled martini glass, garnishing with the frozen blueberry skewer.

*   *   *

"The aroma of this drink is heavenly," **OXFORD HOUSE** *bartender and co-owner Natalie Spak says. "Inevitably, once one is served in our dining room, several more are ordered by neighboring tables within minutes."*

FRENCH FATTY

- 2 OUNCES CALVADOS (BOULARD OR OTHER VSOP)
- 1 OUNCE DOMAINE DE CANTON LIQUEUR
- 2 DASHES BITTERS
- 1 DASH SIMPLE SYRUP*
- 3+OUNCES FATTY BAMPKINS HARD CIDER
- 2 TABLESPOONS CINNAMON SUGAR
- DRIED APPLE CHIP

Chill a martini glass, then wet its rim. Spread the cinnamon sugar around the edge of a small saucer, and create a rim by upending the chilled glass into the sugar. Put the calvados, Domaine de Canton, bitters, and simple syrup into a cocktail shaker, add ice. Shake. Strain carefully into the martini glass, topping with the hard cider and garnishing with the apple chip.

*   *   *

Get in the mood for a Portland First Friday art walk with a little French influence. Have a French Fatty, choose one of **PETITE JACQUELINE'S** *authentic 3-course bistro prix fixes with some vin rouge, and you'll walk out happy as a clam, ready for your beret fitting.*

BLUE BASIL

MAKES TWO DRINKS:

- 6 BASIL LEAVES
- ½ CUP WYMAN'S WILD BLUEBERRIES
- SPLASH OF SIMPLE SYRUP* (OR MORE TO TASTE)
- 3½ OUNCES VODKA
- BIG SPLASH OF WINTERPORT WINERY BLUEBERRY WINE
- SPLASH OF SODA WATER

In a cocktail shaker, muddle the basil with the blueberries and mix in simple syrup and vodka. Fill two chilled Collins glasses half full with ice, divide contents of shaker equally between them, and finish with a generous splash of Winterport Winery blueberry wine and a splash of soda water.

*   *   *

Winterport Winery's blueberry wine and Wyman's wild Maine blueberries are exactly the kind of SUPER local ingredients **TRATTORIA ATHENA** *prides itself in using, particularly because both are found nowhere else. This is just the smallest part of the effort Chefs Tim and Marc and front-of-house cruise director, Michelle, make to showcase Maine's talents, from glass to plate, aperitif to dessert and everything in between.*

WINTERPORT WINERY & PENOBSCOT BAY BREWERY

WINTERPORT

When Joan Anderson gave her husband, Mike, a home winemaking kit 40 years ago, she never imagined that today, the couple would be at the head of a business producing 17 different wines and 7 beers, and employing almost the entire family. Nestled into the small village of Winterport overlooking Penobscot Bay, Winterport Winery has become a favorite stop for summer visitors and locals alike.

"Winemaking," Mike says, "started as a creative outlet and it still is. We make very high quality wines, almost all of them with local and New England fruits, which just makes sense, using Maine apples for our apple wine and blueberries for that wine. Of course, people see the word 'winery' and don't always think that it's made from fruit." He acknowledges that "the hurdle is higher with fruit wines, but then all we have to do is have people taste 'em. A dry white wine made from pears, a dry blueberry wine, it's not what they expect."

Joan runs the tasting room, welcoming groups large and small. "Most often," she says, "they're surprised, surprised that our dry wines are actually quite dry and that not everything is a dessert wine. Part of what I do in the tasting room is to help them discover and explore, helping them to see that our wines are made, as Mike always says, to be enjoyed with good food and good friends."

The natural extension of this thinking led to Pairings, the airy upstairs space that is part teaching kitchen, part private event space, host to food and wine themed pairing meals, corporate team building workshops, and laid back beer and wine tastings throughout the year.

Scratching another itch a few years ago, Mike started small batch brewing, a sideline that has grown to seven year-round and seasonal offerings embracing

beer styles familiar and not so. "It started out as something I had to do to fill a technicality in the law," he says, "but it just took off. Now, it's just a natural with everything else we do."

What's next for Winterport? Ice cream. (You'll just have to stop by and ask Mike or Joan how *that* happened!)

WINTER

NORTH WOODS

- 1 ounce Bulleit Rye
- 1 ounce Bartlett Fine Apple Brandy
- ¾ ounce Benedictine
- ¼ ounce green Chartreuse
- ½ ounce fresh lemon juice
- ½ ounce Maine maple syrup
- 1 dash Sweetgrass Farm Cranberry Bitters
- Lemon peel twist garnish

Fill a martini glass with ice and water to chill. Place all ingredients in a cocktail shaker with ice. Empty martini glass. Shake cocktail shaker and strain into the martini glass. Garnish with the lemon twist. Barkeep Stella says, "the drink should not be pink – just a dash of the bitters will do, thank you."

*   *   *

At **BAR LOLA** *atop Portland's Munjoy Hill, Stella's approach to mixing drinks is just as precise and demanding as her husband, Guy's, is to working the stove. Between the two, you're sure to come away not just satisfied, but feeling fat, sassy, and spoiled into the bargain!*

THE DEAD LETTER OFFICE

- ¾ OUNCE RYE WHISKEY
- ¾ OUNCE Luxardo MARASCHINO CHERRY LIQUEUR
- ¾ OUNCE LEMON JUICE
- GREEN CHARTREUSE TO RINSE
- 3+ OUNCES ALLAGASH CURIEUX BOURBON BARREL AGED STRONG ALE

Chill a cocktail glass. In a cocktail shaker, mix the rye, Luxardo, and lemon juice and shake. Pour just enough green chartreuse in the chilled glass to coat it while swirling. Dump remaining chartreuse. Strain the mixture from the cocktail shaker into the glass. Top with 3+ ounces Allagash Curieux.

*   *   *

If this drink doesn't make you "curieux" about **BLACK BIRCH***, you need to have another. Seriously, with a turntable and stack of vinyls behind the bar and a finely-tuned 19th-century sensibility in the atmosphere and drink list, this is a joint not to miss.*

A.G.A. COCKTAIL

- 2½ ounces Aquavit
- ¾ ounce ginger wild blueberry cardamom syrup*
- 2 teaspoons freshly squeezed lemon juice
- 1 dash Angostura Bitters
- 3-4 Maine blueberries
- 1 cocktail spear

Chill a cocktail glass. Put the aquavit, ginger syrup, and bitters in a mixing glass. Fill it with ice, shake, and double strain into chilled cocktail glass. To double strain, use a standard Hawthorne strainer on the mixing glass and pour from that through a tea strainer into the cocktail glass. Pierce 3-4 Maine blueberries with a cocktail spear for garnish.

*   *   *

The **BLUE SPOON** *is not just another cozy joint up on Munjoy Hill. It is the cozy joint, either for a gorgeous small-plate lunch or for a more lively eve when, it seems, half the neighborhood often just decides to show up, too, for one of their signature cocktails and a bite or two to go with.*

GINGER HOT TODDY

- ½" PIECE OF GINGER, PEELED AND DICED
- 3 OUNCES CINNAMON-INFUSED BOURBON*
- 6 OUNCES HOT WATER
- 1 TEASPOON+ URBAN FARM FERMENTORY BLUEBERRY BLOSSOM HONEY
- LEMON SLICE

Preheat a tall glass mug by filling it with hot water. In a tall mixing cup, muddle ginger well then add bourbon. Let sit 1 minute to infuse. Empty glass mug and add honey and 1 ounce of hot water, stirring to combine. Strain the bourbon-ginger mix into a separate glass, then strain again into glass mug. Add remaining hot water and garnish with lemon slice. Some people like more honey.

*   *   *

BODA'S *Thai owners, Bob and Dan, were very likely the first to bring cinnamon-infused bourbon—along with a host of flavors from the mother country—to Portland. With just a hint of honey and ginger, this toddy is a true winter warmer.*

TURBO DIESEL

- 1½ OUNCES BARTLETT FINE APPLE BRANDY
- 1 OUNCE AGED RUM
- ½ TEASPOON SUGAR
- 2-3 DASHES SWEETGRASS FARM CRANBERRY BITTERS
- ½ LIME
- ¼ LEMON
- JALAPEÑO SLICE, PICKLED OR FRESH

In a tumbler add sugar and bitters. Fill half with ice, and into this squeeze juice from the lemon and lime. Add brandy and rum. Shake to the Bossa Nova for 10 seconds. Strain into a cocktail glass and garnish with jalapeño ring floating on top.

*   *   *

A big jar of pickled jalapeños sits on the bar at **EL CAMINO,** *ready for just such an occasion. Add to this the brandy, rum, and bitters, and the Turbo packs enough punch to kick you right into spring.*

URBAN FARM FERMENTORY

PORTLAND

If you can get Eli Cayer, founder of Urban Farm Fermentory in Portland, to sit still for a minute, he'll come right out and tell you, "Our business plan? We're going to ferment *everything we can get locally and get people engaged in recycling waste streams!*"

His interest in community and a chance encounter with bee keeping led him first to ferment honey to create mead. Over time this evolved into fermenting apples into hard cider and cabbage into sauerkraut. This last bit really opened his eyes to the health benefits of lacto-fermented and seasonal foods.

One thing is certain, this place is alive. After barely a year in the market; the Urban Farm Fermentory brand and it's CULTURE product line have taken off like a rocket.

There are also pleasantly rustic yet urban designed hard ciders, meads, kombuchas, specialty vinegars, and infused raw honey cultures.

Walk into the 2500-square-foot space and the senses are assaulted by stimuli coming from every direction. First, there's the intense overlay of fermentation funk, then the visual chaos of recycled and repurposed materials, urban art, the seeming confusion of pipes, barrels, tanks, tubing, bottles, jugs, and then the various sounds of production overlaid with heavy rhythmic beats.

Eli takes the curious visitor from the tasting room, by the mead and cider rooms past a cold room for keg conditioning, intentionally vented so its excess heat warms the kombucha fermentation room next to it. Here a back door opens onto a long stretch of south–facing open space, an abandoned rail bed. Eli reclaimed and developed this area with partner and permaculture designer/workshop coordinator, David Homa.

Here, raised beds and vertical grow space dominate. Basking in the sun sit a

couple of greenhouses. One, built as a collaboration with biologist Tyler Gaudett, is fitted with a clever tilapia mini-aquaculture system. In this closed loop design, the water is continuously filtered as it flows through and nourishes carefully engineered beds of microgreens and herbs before flowing back to the fish.

Beyond this, beehives. "Last year," Eli points out, "the bees made a fantastic honey from that Japanese knotweed," a common weed in this overgrown, semi-abandoned industrial space. Who knows what you might find next year?

Real, healthy, experimental—that's the Urban Farm Fermentory.

APPLE HOT TODDY

- 2 OUNCES MAINE MEAD WORKS APPLE CYSER MEAD
- 1½ OUNCES BARTLETT'S FINE APPLE BRANDY
- 1 TEASPOON MAINE WILDFLOWER HONEY
- 2 OUNCES BOILING WATER
- 4-5 DASHES SWEETGRASS FARM CRANBERRY OR OTHER BITTERS
- FRESH APPLE SLICE

Combine first three ingredients in a small pitcher, stir, heat to steaming. Pour into a clear, glass mug, top with boiling water, add the dashes of bitters. Garnish with apple slice and serve.

*   *   *

FIVE FIFTY FIVE *restaurant melds three distinctive Maine flavors—apples, cranberry, and honey—into a satisfying hot brew with that hint of fire from the apple brandy sure to stimulate the blood as well as the appetite.*

QUEEN BEE

- 1½ ounces Glenmorangie or other mild Highland Scotch
- 1 ounce HoneyMaker Semi-sweet Mead from Maine Mead Works
- ¾ ounce Drambuie
- 1 ounce Earl Grey tea brewed double strength then cooled
- ½ ounce fresh squeezed lemon juice
- 2 dashes Fee Brothers Old-Fashioned Bitters
- Lemon twist for garnish

Combine all ingredients in a large mixing glass. Fill with ice and stir until well-chilled. Strain into a chilled cocktail glass and garnish with the twist of lemon.

*   *   *

Honey, bergamot, Scotch, lemon—all strong flavors intertwined here in such a way as to demand your mouth's attention while your mind says, oh my God is that good! This is in the best **HUGO'S** *tradition, which the new owners have not just adopted but adapted after they took the reins of this venerable Portland culinary destination.*

MACHE 75

- 1 OUNCE COLD RIVER BLUEBERRY VODKA
- 1 OUNCE BLUEBERRY SIMPLE SYRUP*
- 3 | OUNCES CHAMPAGNE OR PROSECCO
- 5 OR 6 WILD MAINE BLUEBERRIES, FRESH OR FROZEN DEPENDING ON SEASON

Drop the berries into a champagne flute, add the vodka and simple syrup then top with champagne or prosecco.

*   *   *

Marie Yarborough, **MACHE'S** *house manager, barkeep, and chef's wife, calls this refresher "Our Maine take on the French 75, the gin, champagne, and lemon juice drink made famous by Harry's New York Bar in Paris around the First World War." Open almost year round, this gem of a bistro has an ambiance that brings local fishermen to the bar elbow to elbow with summer visitors from distant ports. And, yes, it's the food that these strangers are talking about, unfussy local flavors drawn big on the plate by Chef Kyle.*

OLD FASHIONED MAINER MASH

- 5 Maine cranberries
- ½ orange slice
- ½ teaspoon Maine maple sugar
- 1½ ounces Bulleit bourbon
- 1½ ounces Sweetgrass Farm Maine Maple Mash

In the bottom of an old-fashioned glass, muddle cranberries, orange slice, and maple sugar until sugar has dissolved and the fruit juices are released. Fill the glass with ice. Add the bourbon and Maine Maple Mash. Transfer contents of glass to a cocktail shaker and gently shake to combine ingredients. Pour contents back into the old-fashioned glass without straining.

*   *   *

"The Maple Mash," **OXFORD HOUSE** *barkeep and co-owner Natalie Spak says, "adds just a hint of subtle sweetness at the end of a sip to this rustic yet complexly delicate cocktail. Best enjoyed in front of a crackling fire on a snowy night."*

LE COCKTAIL MYRTILLE-POMME

- 1 OUNCE WYMAN'S WILD BLUEBERRY JUICE
- 1 OUNCE MAINE APPLE CIDER
- 1 OUNCE COGNAC
- SPLASH OF FRESH-SQUEEZED LEMON JUICE
- LEMON TWIST

Combine blueberry juice, cider, cognac, and lemon juice in a rocks glass. Stir and garnish with a twist of lemon.

*　　*　　*

Sometimes, simple is best, here showcasing two signature Maine ingredients, wild blueberries and apple cider, with just a touch of alcohol and bit of citrus to bring out the best in each. This laid-back, unadorned approach is also apparent in PETITE JACQUELINE'S *bistro plates, none of which would look out of place on the table at a rustic joint along the Boul Mich in Paris. Santé!*

RED SKY DARK & STORMY

- 2½ OUNCES GOSLING'S BLACK SEAL RUM
- 5½ OUNCES MAINE ROOT GINGER BEER
- 1 TEASPOON FRESH GINGER JUICE
- LIME TWIST FOR GARNISH

Fill a Collins glass with ice, add the rum and ginger juice then top with ginger beer. Stir once or twice. Garnish with lime twist and serve.

*　　*　　*

"At Red Sky," said Elizabeth Lindquist, who owns **RED SKY** *with her husband, James, "we really like our ginger. Here, the fresh ginger juice offsets the sweetness of the rum."*
Their restaurant, tucked away in the compact village of Southwest Harbor, is a refuge open almost year round, always welcoming to strangers and regulars alike with an inventive and spirited menu offering much local and from the sea.

GLOSSARY OF BAR PREPS, SIMPLE SYRUPS, AND INFUSED ALCOHOLS

ANCHO CHILI/HIBISCUS INFUSED TEQUILA

In a 2-liter infusing jar, add one liter white tequila (not too expensive) and 1 to 1½ cups dried hibiscus flowers. Let sit for 2-3 days, until flavor is tart and satisfactory. Strain out hibiscus flowers and add 2 dried, deseeded ancho chilis torn into pieces. Taste tequila after twelve hours at regular intervals until you can taste the smoke and spice, usually not longer than 24 hours total. Strain and enjoy.

BASIL SIMPLE SYRUP

Wash and dry basil. (Don't bother removing leaves from stems. Just use a salad spinner.) Bring 1 cup water and 1 cup sugar to a boil, remove from heat. Put the basil in the simple syrup and let stand one hour. Strain out basil. Keep cool.

BLUEBERRY COULIS

Put 1 cup of blueberries, frozen or fresh, ¼ cup of sugar, and 2 teaspoons of lemon juice in a small saucepan and simmer until the berries are soft and the sugar dissolved, about 10 minutes. Taste the sauce, which should be sweet but not overly so. Add more sugar if desired. Strain through a cheesecloth.

BLUEBERRY-THYME SYRUP

In a small saucepan, combine ¼ cup sugar, ¼ cup water, ¼ cup Wyman's frozen wild blueberries, 1 sprig fresh thyme, and the juice and peel of a fat slice of lemon. Stir over medium heat until mixture boils, then strain through a fine sieve, pressing blueberries with the back of a spoon to extract all of their flavor and juice.

BLUEBERRY SIMPLE SYRUP

Combine 1 cup water, ½ cup sugar, the juice of ½ lemon, and ¼ cup dried or ½ cup wild Maine blueberries (Wyman's is always available frozen) in a small saucepan. Simmer 5 minutes then allow to cool. Strain.

BROWN SIMPLE SYRUP

Dissolve ½ cup brown sugar in ½ cup hot water.

CANDIED ROSEMARY

Take a sprig of fresh rosemary, dip it in simple syrup then roll it in sugar, shaking off excess.

CILANTRO SYRUP

In a small saucepan bring a cup of water and a cup of sugar to a boil. Add one bunch (about one cup crammed) cilantro, stems and all, and reduce heat, simmering 30 minutes. Cover and let cool, then strain and refrigerate.

CINNAMON-INFUSED BOURBON

In a dry saucepan, toast 1 small cinnamon stick until just slightly charred. Add to 12 ounces bourbon and let sit 24-48 hours. Remove cinnamon.

CRANBERRY SIMPLE SYRUP

Put 2 12-ounce bags Maine cranberries (fresh is best), 2 cups water, and 1⅓ cups sugar into a small saucepan, turn heat to medium, and boil. Reduce heat, simmering 15-20 minutes or until the cranberries have burst. Strain through a sieve into a medium bowl, pressing gently on the berries with the back of a wooden spoon. Cool syrup to room temperature. Keeps, refrigerated, up to two weeks.

FIDDLEHEAD HOUSE PICKLE

This recipe is for fiddleheads, but we use it also with green beans, Brussels sprouts, and cornichon cucumbers. Blanch 6 cups cleaned fiddleheads or other vegetable. Drain. Put the fiddleheads in a sealable, nonreactive glass or plastic container along with 4-5 cloves minced garlic, 2 teaspoons dill seed, 1 peeled 8" piece of fresh ginger, and 2 tablespoons sambal oelek. Heat the caraway seed and Szechuan peppercorns in a 2-quart saucepan until aromatic, then add 3 cups water, 3 cups rice wine vinegar, and ½ cup sugar. Simmer to steep, then cool. Pour over fiddlehead mixture, cover, and refrigerate. This will keep, covered and cooled, up to 2 weeks in the refrigerator. If you see any sign of sliminess or unpleasant odor, discard and start again.

GINGER SYRUP

Peel and slice thinly ¼ cup of fresh gingerroot. Simmer ginger with 4 black peppercorns, ½ cup sugar, and ½ cup water until syrup is flavorful and reduced, about 30 minutes. Strain and reserve peppercorns and ginger slices for garnish, if using in next few days.

GINGER WILD BLUEBERRY CARDAMOM SYRUP

Put 2 cups water and ½ cup sugar in a small saucepan. Boil. Reduce to low heat and add 1 tablespoon of cracked cardamom seeds and ¾ ounce of peeled fresh ginger in thin slices. Simmer for 10 minutes then cool. Strain off ginger and cardamom, then add 2 pints Maine wild blueberries and muddle. Strain through a moistened cheese cloth and squeeze to extract final drops of blueberry juice. Strain this through a tea strainer, then refrigerate.

LAVENDER-INFUSED TRIPLE SEC

Soak 2 tablespoons of dried lavender flowers in triple sec for at least 2 days. Strain and reserve liquid.

LEMON- AND ROEMARY-INFUSED VODKA

Zest 2 lemons, reserve. Remove pith and skin from the lemons and slice finely. In an infusion jar, add lemons and zest along with 6 sprigs fresh rosemary to 1 liter medium-quality unflavored vodka. Let sit for three days, stirring daily. Strain.

MAPLE CLOVE SYRUP

Bring a cup of water and 2 teaspoons whole cloves to boil in a small saucepan. Remove from heat, cover, steep for half and hour. Strain off the cloves. Measure the remaining liquid and add an equal amount of the Maine maple syrup. This should be enough for at least 6 drinks.

MARINATED OLIVES

Put a handful of Alfonso and a handful of Kalamata olives in a 1 pint container with a tightly fitting lid. Cover with dry vermouth and add 2 tablespoons each crushed dry sage and thyme. Marinate for at least seven days, shaking container once each day.

RASPBERRY SIMPLE SYRUP

In a small saucepan put a pint of fresh raspberries, ½ cup sugar, one cinnamon stick, and the zest of one orange. Simmer until thick and syrupy. Strain through a sieve, pressing berries with the back of a spoon, and chill liquid.

RASPBERRY-INFUSED VODKA

Put 5 pints of fresh raspberries, rinsed and gently shaken dry, into an infusion jar with 1 liter of vodka and let stand 3-5 days. Smaller batch: 2 pints raspberries and 1 pint vodka. You can leave the raspberries in the vodka as long as there is enough alcohol to cover them.

RHUBARB SIMPLE SYRUP

In a small sauce pan, put a cup of granulated sugar, a cup of water, and 6-8 ounces of rhubarb stalks cut into ¼" chunks. Bring to a boil, reduce to simmer, 20-25 minutes. Strain. Cool. If you use green stalks of rhubarb, your syrup will be almost clear. If you use the red stalks, it will be slightly pink.

ROSEMARY-INFUSED HONEY

Put 4 or 5 sprigs of rosemary in a pint jar of honey and let sit for several days at least. Remove rosemary sprigs.

SIMPLE SYRUP

Heat equal parts plain white sugar and water in a saucepan over medium heat until sugar is dissolved. Cool.

SMOKY APPLE-INFUSED VODKA

Core 4 Liberty apples but peel only in alternating stripes. The flesh will hold the smoke while the remaining peel imparts more apple flavor. First cold-smoke the apples in a smoker or grill at 150°F for 1-2 hours. Apples should still be firm. Put the reserved lemons and apples from **SMOKY LEMON SIMPLE SYRUP** *(see below) into 1 liter Twenty-2 vodka and infuse 3-5 days at room temperature.*

SMOKY LEMON SIMPLE SYRUP

Combine 1 quart water and 2 cups granulated sugar in a saucepan and simmer until sugar is dissolved. When cool add 4 smoked apples (see **SMOKY APPLE-INFUSED VODKA**) and 2 lemons in slices and soak overnight. Remove apples and lemons and reserve and strain syrup. Keep cold.

SOUR MIX FROM FRONTIER

For 3 cups of sour mix: in a one-quart glass container, put 1 cup fresh-squeezed lime juice, 1 cup fresh-squeezed lemon juice, and 1 cup simple syrup (see above). Into this grate the zest of 1 lime. Let sit several hours, in the refrigerator.

SPICY HERBED TOMATO WATER

In the bowl of a food processor put: 2 Olivia's Garden tomatoes chopped roughly, 2 tablespoons fresh chopped rosemary, 2 tablespoons finely chopped thyme, 1 tablespoon prepared horseradish, 2 dashes Tabasco Sauce, 1 teaspoon kosher salt, and 1 teaspoon fresh ground black pepper. Purée all ingredients. Strain through mesh strainer using a ladle to force juices through until only pulp is left in strainer. Refrigerate.

STRAWBERRY-INFUSED TEQUILA

Wash and hull a pint of local strawberries, then slice them. Soak the strawberry slices in your choice of 100% agave tequila for at least two days. Strain and reserve liquid.

THYME SIMPLE SYRUP

In a small saucepan bring 1 cup water and 1 cup granulated sugar to a gentle boil until sugar is dissolved. Remove from heat and add 4-5 sprigs fresh thyme. Steep for ten minutes, remove thyme, then chill. Keeps two weeks refrigerated.

INDEX OF COCKTAILS
BY RESTAURANT & PRODUCER

INDEX OF FEATURED ARTISAN PRODUCERS

CONTACT INFORMATION FOR RESTAURANTS

ANNEKE JANS, *www.annekejans.net*

BAR LOLA, *www.barlola.net*

BLACK BIRCH, *www.theblackbirch.com*

BLUE SPOON, *http://bluespoonme.com*

BODA, *www.bodamaine.com*

CAIOLA'S, *http://caiolas.com*

EAST ENDER, *http://eastenderportland.com*

EL CAMINO CANTINA, *www.elcaminomaine.com*

EVENTIDE OYSTER HOUSE, *www.hugos.net*

FIDDLEHEAD RESTAURANT, *www.thefidldlcheadrcstaurant.com*

50 LOCAL, *www.localkennebunk.com*

FISHBONES AMERICAN GRILL, *www.fishbonesag.com*

FIVE FIFTY FIVE, *http://fivefifty-five.com*

FORE STREET RESTAURANT, *www.forestreet.biz*

FRANCINE BISTRO, *www.francinebistro.com*

THE FROG AND TURTLE, *www.thefrogandturtle.com*

FRONTIER, *www.explorefrontier.com*

HUGO'S RESTAURANT, *www.hugos.net*

JOSHUA'S RESTAURANT, *http://joshuas.biz*

MACHE BISTRO, *http://machebistro.com*

OXFORD HOUSE INN, *www.oxfordhouseinn.com*

PETITE JACQUELINE, *http://bistropj.com*

RED SKY, *http://redskyrestaurant.com*

SEAGRASS BISTRO, *www.seagrassbistro.com*

SHERPHERD'S PIE, *www.shepherdspierockport.com*

SOLO BISTRO, *www.solobistro.com*

TRATTORIA ATHENA, *www.trattoriaathena.com*

VIGNOLA, *www.vignolamaine.com*

ZAPOTECA, *www.zapotecarestaurant.com*

CONTACT INFORMATION FOR FEATURED ARTISAN PRODUCERS

Allagash Brewing, tasting room and brewery tours, FMI: www.allagash.com

Bar Harbor Foods, FMI: www.barharborfoods.com

Bartlett Maine Estate Winery and Spirits of Maine Distillery, tasting room, FMI: www.bartlettwinery.com

Maine Mead Works, tasting room, FMI: www.mainemeadworks.com

Sweetgrass Farm Winery and Distillery, tasting room, FMI: www.sweetgrasswinery.com

Urban Farm Fermentory, tasting room, classes, FMI: www.urbanfarmfermentory.com

Winterport Winery and Penobscot Bay Brewery, tasting room, tasting meals, FMI: www.winterportwinery.com

Wyman's of Maine, FMI: www.wymans.com

HOW THIS BOOK WAS PRODUCED

DRINKING IN MAINE is a collaboration of writer Michael Sanders, photographer Russell French, and more than 30 very dedicated Maine bartenders and restaurateurs up and down the coast and inland. To make this the best book possible, we borrowed a page from the Slow Food ethos, asking eight carefully chosen artisan producers—Allagash Brewing, Bar Harbor Foods, Bartlett Maine Estate Winery and Spirits of Maine Distillery, Maine Mead Works, Sweetgrass Farm Winery and Distillery, Urban Farm Fermentory, Winterport Winery, and Wyman's of Maine—to become co-producers with us, contributing to the production costs of the book.

Change comes to the business of food and drink with a particular vengeance, which is why every edition of this book will be a new one. We welcome your feedback, your thoughts, and ideas for artisan producers and restaurants who should be a part of this evolving project. Please contact us through the website: www.tableartsmedia.com, putting the word "feedback" in the subject line.